whoopie pies

whoopie pies

30 recipes for treats for every occasion

First published in 2011
LOVE FOOD is an imprint of Parragon Books Ltd

Parragon
Queen Street House
4 Queen Street
Bath BA1 1HE, UK

ISBN: 978-1-4454-2877-2

Printed in China

Written by Angela Drake
Photography by Clive Streeter
Home economy and food styling by Angela Drake

Notes for the Reader
This book uses imperial, metric, and US cup measurements. Follow the same units of measurement throughout; do not mix imperial and metric. All spoon measurements are level: teaspoons are assumed to be 5 ml, and tablespoons are assumed to be 15 ml. Unless otherwise stated, milk is assumed to be whole, eggs and individual vegetables, such as potatoes, are medium, and pepper is freshly ground black pepper.

The times given are an approximate guide only. Preparation times differ according to the techniques used by different people and the cooking times may also vary from those given as a result of the type of oven used. Optional ingredients, variations, or serving suggestions have not been included in the calculations.

Recipes using raw or very lightly cooked eggs should be avoided by infants, the elderly, pregnant women, convalescents, and anyone with a chronic condition. Pregnant and breast-feeding women are advised to avoid eating peanuts and peanut products. People with nut allergies should be aware that some of the prepared ingredients used in the recipes in this book may contain nuts. Always check the packaging before use.

Contents

JUST WHAT IS A WHOOPIE PIE?

Simple to make and delicious to eat, a whoopie pie is two soft mounds of cake sandwiched together with a creamy filling to make a perfect handheld sweet treat! An American invention, legend has it that the name "whoopie pie" comes from the cry of "Whoopie!" that farmers or children would shout when they opened their lunch boxes and found one nestling inside. The traditional and original whoopie pie consists of two dark and moist chocolate cakes filled with a generous amount of creamy white marshmallow frosting. Other classic flavors include vanilla, pumpkin, chocolate chip, and gingerbread, but there's no limit to the variety of flavors and fillings that can be created. In this book, you'll find a huge selection of whoopie pie recipes, ranging from classic favorites to deliciously overindulgent versions for extra special occasions. You don't need to have the skills of a master baker to produce great whoopie pies, and you'll find that once you enter the world of whoopie pie making, there'll be no going back!

EQUIPMENT YOU WILL NEED

Baking sheets: It's worth investing in 2–3 large, good-quality baking sheets for making whoopie pies. As a general guide, you'll be able to fit only 8–10 mounds of the mixture on each sheet (more for the miniature whoopies) because you need to allow plenty of room for the mixture to spread during baking. Line the sheets with nonstick parchment paper.

Measuring spoons and cups: These are necessary for accurate measuring.

Electric handheld mixer: Although not essential, you'll save time and energy by using a handheld electric mixer for the first stages of making the whoopie pie mixture.

Flexible plastic spatula: A rubber or silicone spatula with a firm handle is ideal for scraping the mixture down the sides of the bowl and making sure all the dry ingredients are thoroughly incorporated. It's also great to use when filling pastry bags with the cake mixture or filling.

Pastry bag and tips: To get even, round whoopie pies, it's best to pipe the mixture onto the baking sheets. Use a large nylon, fabric, or disposable plastic pastry bag fitted with a large, plain piping tip.

Large and small palette knives: Use a large palette knife to transfer the whoopie pies to a cooling rack. A small palette knife is perfect for spreading filling or frosting onto the baked whoopies.

INGREDIENTS FOR THE TASTIEST WHOOPIES

Butter: Although many American recipes use vegetable shortening to make whoopie pies, most of the recipes in this book are made with butter, which produces a richer flavor and a slightly firmer cake that is easier to fill. Use lightly salted butter and let it soften at room temperature before using. For buttercream, use an unsalted butter.

Vegetable shortening: A soft, white flavorless fat, it is creamed with butter in some of the recipes to create lighter, more crumbly textured cakes. Vegetable shortening is available in most grocery stores.

Sugar: Use superfine sugar for pale or delicately flavored whoopie pies, such as lemon or vanilla. Light and dark brown sugars are best for whoopie pies with stronger flavorings, such as chocolate and ginger.

Eggs: Remove eggs from the refrigerator 1 hour before using them.

Flour and leavening agents: White or whole wheat all-purpose flour is used to make whoopie pies with the addition of baking soda or baking powder as the leavening agent. Be careful when measuring the leavening agent because too much may cause the cakes to collapse when they come out of the oven.

Milk, sour cream, and cultured buttermilk: The liquid element of the whoopie pie mixture, these acidic liquids help to create a chemical reaction with the leavening agent to create light and airy cakes.

Vanilla extract: An essential flavoring in many of the whoopie pies—make sure you buy the real thing for the best flavor.

TOP TIPS FOR MAKING WONDERFUL WHOOPIES

- If the creamed mixture begins to curdle a little when you add the egg, stir in a spoonful of the sifted flour mixture.
- Piping the whoopie pie mixture onto the baking sheets will ensure fairly evenly shaped rounds, but using a tablespoon or small ice-cream scoop will work just as well. Try to keep the mounds as round as possible and don't be tempted to spread or flatten them.
- Remember oven temperatures can vary considerably. Convection ovens cook more quickly than conventional ovens, so reduce the temperature by 50°F/10°C. Check the whoopie pies after about 6–8 minutes.
- To check if the whoopie pies are cooked, lightly press the top of one with your fingertip—if the pie springs back, it's ready; if it leaves a slight indentation, then return to the oven for another couple of minutes.

- Don't be tempted to transfer the whoopies pies to a cooling rack as soon as they come out of the oven. They need at least 5 minutes to let them firm up and cool slightly.
- However neatly you piped or spooned the mixture onto the baking sheets, you will probably still find slight variations in the shapes and sizes of the baked whoopie pies. This is not a problem—just match them up accordingly when pairing them together before filling.
- To fill a whoopie pie, pipe a large swirl or drop a heaped spoonful of the filling onto the center of one cake. Place a second cake on top and press down gently. If the filling is a little soft, chill the filled pies in the refrigerator for 1–2 hours.
- To freeze unfilled whoopie pies, spread them on a baking sheet and freeze—without covering—until solid, then pack them interleaved with parchment paper in freezer containers or bags and store in the freezer. To defrost, spread the frozen whoopie pies in a single layer on baking sheets and let stand at room temperature for 1–2 hours.
- Filled whoopie pies are best eaten on the day of filling; however, they will keep for up to 2–3 days in an airtight container. Whoopie pies with a cream or cream cheese filling should be kept in the refrigerator, but remove them and let stand at room temperature for 30 minutes before serving.
- Finally, don't be afraid to experiment—once you've enjoyed a few of these whoopie pie recipes, why not try your own flavor variation or mix and match the different fillings and toppings? The permutations are endless!
- Above all, have fun making whoopies!!!

Classic Whoopie

chocolate whoopie pies

makes 10

1¼ cups all-purpose flour

1½ tsp baking soda

scant ½ cup unsweetened cocoa

large pinch of salt

6 tbsp butter, softened

generous ⅓ cup vegetable shortening

¾ cup dark brown sugar

1 large egg, beaten

1 tsp vanilla extract

⅔ cup milk

marshmallow filling

8 oz/225 g white marshmallows

4 tbsp milk

½ cup vegetable shortening

½ cup confectioners' sugar, sifted

Preheat the oven to 350°F/180°C. Line 2–3 large cookie sheets with parchment paper. Sift together the all-purpose flour, baking soda, unsweetened cocoa, and salt.

Place the butter, vegetable shortening, and sugar in a large bowl and beat with an electric mixer until pale and fluffy. Beat in the egg and vanilla extract followed by half of the flour mixture and then the milk. Stir in the rest of the flour mixture and mix until thoroughly incorporated.

Pipe or spoon 20 mounds of the batter onto the prepared cookie sheets, spaced well apart to allow for spreading. Bake in the preheated oven, one sheet at a time, for 12–14 minutes until risen and just firm to the touch. Cool for 5 minutes, then using a palette knife transfer to a cooling rack and let cool completely.

For the filling, place the marshmallows and milk in a heatproof bowl set over a pan of simmering water. Heat until the marshmallows have melted, stirring occasionally. Remove from the heat and let cool.

Place the vegetable shortening and confectioners' sugar in a bowl and beat together until smooth and creamy. Add the creamed mixture to the marshmallow and beat for 1–2 minutes until fluffy.

To assemble, spread the filling over the flat side of half the cakes. Top with the remaining cakes.

vanilla whoopie pies

makes 12

generous 1¾ cups all-purpose flour

1 tsp baking soda

large pinch of salt

½ cup butter, softened

¾ cup superfine sugar

1 large egg, beaten

2 tsp vanilla extract

⅔ cup buttermilk

chocolate buttercream filling

4 oz/115 g milk chocolate, broken into pieces

¾ cup unsalted butter, softened

2 cups confectioners' sugar, sifted

Preheat the oven to 350°F/180°C. Line 2–3 large cookie sheets with parchment paper. Sift together the all-purpose flour, baking soda, and salt.

Place the butter and sugar in a large bowl and beat with an electric mixer until pale and fluffy. Beat in the egg and vanilla extract followed by half of the flour mixture and then the buttermilk. Stir in the rest of the flour mixture and mix until thoroughly incorporated.

Pipe or spoon 24 mounds of the batter onto the prepared cookie sheets, spaced well apart to allow for spreading. Bake in the preheated oven, one sheet at a time, for 10–12 minutes until risen and just firm to the touch. Cool for 5 minutes, then using a palette knife transfer to a cooling rack and let cool completely.

For the filling, place the chocolate in a heatproof bowl set over a pan of simmering water (make sure the bottom of the bowl does not touch the water) and leave until melted. Remove from the heat and let cool for 20 minutes, stirring occasionally. Place the butter in a bowl and beat with an electric mixer for 2–3 minutes until pale and creamy. Gradually beat in the confectioners' sugar, then beat in the chocolate.

To assemble, spread or pipe the buttercream on the flat side of half of the cakes. Top with the rest of the cakes.

red velvet whoopie pies

makes 10

scant 1½ cups all-purpose flour

1½ tsp baking soda

¼ cup unsweetened cocoa

large pinch of salt

6 tbsp butter, softened

generous ⅓ cup vegetable shortening

¾ cup light brown sugar

1 large egg, beaten

1 tsp vanilla extract

1 tbsp red food coloring

⅔ cup sour cream

vanilla filling

1 cup full-fat cream cheese, at room temperature

4 tbsp unsalted butter, softened

few drops vanilla extract

¾ cup confectioners' sugar, sifted

Preheat the oven to 350°F/180°C. Line 2–3 large cookie sheets with parchment paper. Sift together the all-purpose flour, baking soda, unsweetened cocoa, and salt.

Place the butter, vegetable shortening and sugar in a large bowl and beat with an electric mixer until pale and fluffy. Beat in the egg, vanilla extract, and food coloring followed by half of the flour mixture and then the sour cream. Stir in the rest of the flour mixture and mix until thoroughly incorporated.

Pipe or spoon 20 mounds of the batter onto the prepared cookie sheets, spaced well apart to allow for spreading. Bake, one sheet at a time, in the preheated oven for 12–14 minutes until risen and just firm to the touch. Cool for 5 minutes, then using a palette knife transfer to a cooling rack and let cool completely.

For the filling, place the cream cheese and butter in a bowl and beat together until well blended. Beat in the vanilla extract and confectioners' sugar until smooth.

To assemble, spread or pipe the filling over the flat side of half the cakes. Top with the rest of the cakes.

oatmeal & raisin whoopie pies

makes 12

generous 1¾ cups all-purpose flour

2 tsp baking powder

large pinch of salt

1 tsp apple pie spice

½ cup butter, softened

¾ cup light brown sugar

1 large egg, beaten

⅔ cup milk

1 cup rolled oats

⅓ cup raisins

orange buttercream filling

½ cup unsalted butter, softened

finely grated rind and juice from 1 orange

1¾ cups confectioners' sugar

Preheat the oven to 350°F/180°C. Line 2–3 large cookie sheets with parchment paper. Sift together the all-purpose flour, baking powder, salt, and apple pie spice.

Place the butter and sugar in a large bowl and beat with an electric mixer until pale and fluffy. Beat in the egg followed by half of the flour mixture and then the milk. Stir in the rest of the flour mixture and mix until thoroughly incorporated. Stir in the rolled oats and raisins.

Pipe or spoon 24 mounds of the batter onto the prepared cookie sheets, spaced well apart to allow for spreading. Bake, one sheet at a time, in the preheated oven for 10–12 minutes until risen and just firm to the touch. Cool for 5 minutes, then using a palette knife transfer to a cooling rack and let cool completely.

For the filling, place the butter and orange rind and juice in a bowl and beat with an electric mixer for 2–3 minutes until pale and creamy. Gradually beat in the confectioners' sugar and continue beating for 2–3 minutes until the buttercream is very light and fluffy.

To assemble, spread or pipe the buttercream on the flat side of half of the cakes. Top with the rest of the cakes.

pumpkin whoopie pies

makes 12

2 cups all-purpose flour

½ tsp baking powder

½ tsp baking soda

1½ tsp ground cinnamon

¼ tsp salt

1 cup light brown sugar

½ cup sunflower oil

1 large egg, beaten

1 tsp vanilla extract

½ cup canned pumpkin puree

cinnamon & maple filling

1 cup full-fat cream cheese

4 tbsp unsalted butter, softened

2 tbsp maple syrup

1 tsp ground cinnamon

¾ cup confectioners' sugar, sifted

Preheat the oven to 350°F/180°C. Line 2–3 large cookie sheets with parchment paper. Sift together the all-purpose flour, baking powder, baking soda, cinnamon, and salt.

Place the sugar and oil in a large bowl and beat with an electric mixer for 1 minute. Beat in the egg and vanilla extract then the pumpkin puree. Stir in the sifted flour mixture and beat until thoroughly incorporated.

Spoon or pipe 24 mounds of the batter onto the prepared cookie sheets, spaced well apart to allow for spreading. Bake, one sheet at a time, in the preheated oven for 8–10 minutes until risen and just firm to the touch. Cool for 5 minutes, then using a palette knife transfer to a cooling rack and let cool completely.

For the filling, place the cream cheese and butter in a bowl and beat together until well blended. Beat in the maple syrup, cinnamon, and confectioners' sugar until smooth.

To assemble, pipe or spread the filling over the flat side of half the cakes. Top with the remaining cakes.

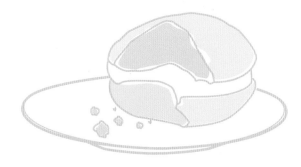

chocolate chip whoopie pies

makes 10

generous 1¾ cups all-purpose flour

1 tsp baking soda

large pinch of salt

½ cup butter, softened

¾ cup light brown sugar

1 large egg, beaten

1 tsp vanilla extract

⅔ cup sour cream

3 oz/85 g semisweet chocolate chips

chocolate filling

5½ oz/150 g semisweet chocolate, broken into pieces

½ cup unsalted butter, softened

⅔ cup heavy cream

Preheat the oven to 350°F/180°C. Line 2–3 large cookie sheets with parchment paper. Sift together the all-purpose flour, baking soda, and salt.

Place the butter and sugar in a large bowl and beat with an electric mixer until pale and fluffy. Beat in the egg and vanilla extract, followed by half of the flour mixture and then the sour cream. Stir in the rest of the flour mixture and mix until thoroughly incorporated. Stir in half of the chocolate chips

Pipe or spoon 20 mounds of the batter onto the prepared cookie sheets, spaced well apart to allow for spreading. Sprinkle over the rest of the chocolate chips. Bake in the preheated oven, one sheet at a time, for 10–12 minutes until risen and just firm to the touch. Cool for 5 minutes, then using a palette knife transfer to a cooling rack and let cool completely.

For the filling, place the chocolate and butter in a heatproof bowl set over a pan of simmering water and heat until melted, stirring occasionally. Remove from the heat and let cool for 20 minutes. Stir the cream into the cooled chocolate, then chill in the refrigerator for 10–15 minutes until firm enough to spread.

To assemble, spread or pipe the chocolate filling on the flat side of half of the cakes. Top with the rest of the cakes.

gingerbread whoopie pies

makes 10

scant 1½ cups all-purpose flour

1½ tsp baking soda

2 tsp ground ginger

¼ tsp salt

5 tbsp butter, softened

generous ⅓ cup vegetable shortening

scant ½ cup dark brown sugar

2 tbsp blackstrap molasses

1 large egg, beaten

generous ⅓ cup milk

ginger cream filling

1 cup full-fat cream cheese

1 cup confectioners' sugar, sifted

4 tbsp heavy cream

2 pieces preserved ginger, finely chopped

Preheat the oven to 350°F/180°C. Line 2–3 large cookie sheets with parchment paper. Sift together the all-purpose flour, baking soda, ginger, and salt.

Place the butter, vegetable shortening and sugar in a large bowl and beat with an electric mixer until pale and fluffy. Beat in the blackstrap molasses and egg followed by half of the flour mixture and then the milk. Stir in the rest of the flour mixture and mix until thoroughly incorporated.

Pipe or spoon 20 mounds of the batter onto the prepared cookie sheets, spaced well apart to allow for spreading. Bake, one sheet at a time, in the preheated oven for 11–13 minutes until risen and just firm to the touch. Cool for 5 minutes, then using a palette knife transfer to a cooling rack and let cool completely.

For the filling, place the cream cheese, confectioners' sugar, and cream in bowl and using an electric mixer, beat together briefly until just smooth. Stir in the preserved ginger.

To assemble, spread the filling over the flat side of half the cakes. Top with the remaining cakes.

peanut butter & jelly whoopie pies

makes 14

generous 1¾ cups all-purpose flour

1 tsp baking soda

large pinch of salt

½ cup butter, softened

¾ cup light brown sugar

1 large egg, beaten

⅔ cup buttermilk

½ cup skinned peanuts, finely ground

1 tbsp roughly chopped salted peanuts

3 tbsp grape jelly

peanut butter buttercream filling

½ cup unsalted butter, softened

½ cup chunky peanut butter

1¼ cups confectioners' sugar, sifted

Preheat the oven to 350°F/180°C. Line 2–3 large baking sheets with baking paper. Sift together the all-purpose flour, baking soda, and salt.

Place the butter and sugar in a large bowl and beat with an electric mixer until pale and fluffy. Beat in the egg, followed by half of the flour mixture and then the buttermilk. Stir in the rest of the flour mixture and mix until thoroughly incorporated. Fold in the ground peanuts.

Pipe or spoon 28 mounds of the mixture onto the prepared baking sheets, spaced well apart to allow for spreading. Sprinkle with the chopped salted nuts. Bake, one sheet at a time, in the preheated oven for 10–12 minutes until risen and just firm to the touch. Cool for 5 minutes, then using a palette knife transfer to a cooling rack and let cool completely.

For the filling, place the butter and peanut butter in a bowl and beat with an electric mixer for 5 minutes until pale and fluffy. Gradually beat in the confectioners' sugar until smooth.

To assemble, spread the buttercream on the flat side of half of the cakes and top with a thin layer of jelly. Top with the rest of the cakes.

Super Whoopie

banana maple cream whoopie pies

makes 12

generous 1¾ cups all-purpose flour

1 tsp baking soda

large pinch of salt

½ cup butter, softened

¾ cup light brown sugar

1 large egg, beaten

generous ⅓ cup buttermilk

1 large ripe banana, peeled and mashed

¾ cup pecans, finely chopped

maple cream filling

1¼ cups heavy cream

3 tbsp maple syrup

Preheat the oven to 350°F/180°C. Line 2–3 large cookie sheets with parchment paper. Sift together the all-purpose flour, baking soda, and salt.

Place the butter and sugar in a large bowl and beat with an electric mixer until pale and fluffy. Beat in the egg followed by half of the flour mixture and then the buttermilk. Stir in the rest of the flour mixture and mix until thoroughly incorporated. Stir in the mashed banana.

Pipe or spoon 24 mounds of the batter onto the prepared cookie sheets, spaced well apart to allow for spreading. Bake in the preheated oven, one sheet at a time, for 10–12 minutes until risen and just firm to the touch. Cool for 5 minutes, then using a palette knife transfer to a cooling rack and let cool completely.

For the filling, place the cream and maple syrup in a bowl and whip together until holding firm peaks.

To assemble, spread or pipe the maple cream on the flat side of half of the cakes. Top with the rest of the cakes. Spread the chopped pecans on a plate and gently roll the edges of each whoopie pie in the nuts to lightly coat.

lucious lemon whoopie pies

makes 10

generous 1¾ cups all-purpose flour

2 tsp baking powder

large pinch of salt

½ cup butter, softened

¾ cup superfine sugar

finely grated rind of 1 lemon

1 large egg, beaten

scant ½ cup milk

4 tbsp lemon curd

1 tbsp yellow sugar sprinkles, to decorate

lemon buttercream filling

½ cup unsalted butter, softened

2 tbsp lemon juice

1¾ cups confectioners' sugar, sifted

icing

1 cup confectioners' sugar

1–2 tbsp warm water

Preheat the oven to 350°F/180°C. Line 2–3 large cookie sheets with parchment paper. Sift together the all-purpose flour, baking powder, and salt.

Place the butter, sugar, and lemon rind in a large bowl and beat with an electric mixer until pale and fluffy. Beat in the egg followed by half of the flour mixture then the milk. Stir in the rest of the flour mixture and beat until thoroughly incorporated.

Pipe or spoon 20 mounds of the batter onto the prepared cookie sheets, spaced well apart to allow for spreading. Bake in the preheated oven, one sheet at a time, for 10–12 minutes until risen and just firm to the touch. Cool for 5 minutes, then using a palette knife transfer to a cooling rack and let cool completely.

For the filling, place the butter and lemon juice in a bowl and beat with an electric mixer for 2–3 minutes until pale and creamy. Gradually beat in the confectioners' sugar and continue beating for 2–3 minutes until the buttercream is very light and fluffy.

For the icing, sift the confectioners' sugar into a bowl and gradually stir in enough water to make a smooth icing that is thick enough to coat the back of a wooden spoon.

To assemble, spread the buttercream on the flat side of half of the cakes and the lemon curd over the other half of the cakes. Sandwich the cakes together. Spoon the icing over the whoopie pies and decorate with sprinkles. Let set.

coconut & raspberry mallow whoopie pies

makes 12

scant 1⅔ cups all-purpose flour

2 tsp baking powder

large pinch of salt

1½ cups dry unsweetened, shredded coconut

½ cup butter, softened

¾ cup superfine sugar

1 large egg, beaten

generous ⅓ cup milk

3 tbsp raspberry jelly

coconut mallow filling

4 oz/115 g white marshmallows

3 tbsp coconut milk

1 cup heavy cream

Preheat the oven to 350°F/180°C. Line 2–3 large cookie sheets with parchment paper. Sift together the all-purpose flour, baking powder, and salt. Stir in half of the coconut. Lightly toast the rest of the coconut and set aside.

Place the butter and sugar in a large bowl and beat with an electric mixer until pale and fluffy. Beat in the egg followed by half of the flour mixture and then the milk. Stir in the rest of the flour mixture and mix until thoroughly incorporated.

Pipe or spoon 24 mounds of the batter onto the prepared cookie sheets, spaced well apart to allow for spreading. Bake in the preheated oven, one sheet at a time, for 10–12 minutes until risen and just firm to the touch. Cool for 5 minutes, then using a palette knife transfer to a cooling rack and let cool completely.

For the filling, place the marshmallows and coconut milk in a heatproof bowl set over a pan of simmering water. Heat until the marshmallows have melted, stirring occasionally. Remove from the heat and let cool. Whip the cream until it holds firm peaks, then fold into the marshmallow mixture. Cover and chill in the refrigerator until firm enough to spread.

To assemble, spread a thin layer of jelly over the flat side of all the cakes. Place a spoonful of the coconut filling on half the cakes and top with the rest. Spread the toasted coconut on a plate and gently roll the edges of each whoopie pie in the coconut to lightly coat.

"be my valentine" whoopie pies

makes 14

generous 1¾ cups all-purpose flour

1 tsp baking soda

large pinch of salt

½ cup butter, softened

¾ cup superfine sugar

1 large egg, beaten

1 tsp vanilla extract

⅔ cup buttermilk

¼ tsp red liquid food coloring

2 tbsp pink heart shaped sugar sprinkles

vanilla buttercream filling

½ cup plus 2 tbsp unsalted butter, softened

1 tsp vanilla extract

4 tbsp heavy cream

2½ cups confectioners' sugar, sifted

icing

1¼ cups confectioners' sugar

1–2 tbsp warm water

few drops red liquid food coloring

Preheat the oven to 350°F/180°C. Line 2–3 large cookie sheets with parchment paper. Sift together the all-purpose flour, baking soda, and salt.

Place the butter and sugar in a large bowl and beat with an electric mixer until pale and fluffy. Beat in the egg and vanilla extract followed by half of the flour mixture and then the buttermilk and food coloring. Stir in the rest of the flour mixture and mix until thoroughly incorporated.

Pipe or spoon 28 mounds of the batter onto the prepared cookie sheets, spaced well apart to allow for spreading. Bake in the preheated oven, one sheet at a time, for 9–11 minutes until risen and just firm to the touch. Cool for 5 minutes, then using a palette knife transfer to a cooling rack and let cool completely.

For the filling, place the butter and vanilla extract in a bowl and beat with an electric mixer for 2–3 minutes until pale and creamy. Beat in the cream, then gradually beat in the confectioners' sugar and continue beating for 2–3 minutes.

For the icing, sift the confectioners' sugar into a bowl and stir in enough water to make a smooth icing that is thick enough to coat the back of a wooden spoon. Beat in a few drops of food coloring to color the icing pale pink.

To assemble, spread or pipe the buttercream on the flat side of half of the cakes. Top with the rest of the cakes. Spoon the icing over the top and decorate with sprinkles. Let set.

double chocolate whoopie pies

makes 12

scant 1½ cups all-purpose flour

1½ tsp baking soda

¼ cup unsweetened cocoa

large pinch of salt

6 tbsp butter, softened

generous ⅓ cup vegetable shortening

¾ cup light brown sugar

1 oz/25 g semisweet chocolate, finely grated

1 large egg, beaten

½ cup milk

4 tbsp semisweet chocolate sprinkles

white chocolate filling

6 oz/175 g white chocolate, broken into pieces

2 tbsp milk

1¼ cups heavy cream

Preheat the oven to 350°F/180°C. Line 2–3 large cookie sheets with parchment paper. Sift together the all-purpose flour, baking soda, unsweetened cocoa, and salt.

Place the butter, vegetable shortening, sugar, and grated chocolate in a large bowl and beat with an electric mixer until pale and fluffy. Beat in the egg followed by half of the flour mixture and then the milk. Stir in the rest of the flour mixture and mix until thoroughly incorporated.

Pipe or spoon 24 mounds of the batter onto the prepared cookie sheets, spaced well apart to allow for spreading. Bake in the preheated oven, one sheet at a time, for 10–12 minutes until risen and just firm to the touch. Cool for 5 minutes, then using a palette knife transfer to a cooling rack and let cool completely.

For the filling, place the chocolate and milk in a heatproof bowl set over a pan of simmering water. Heat until the chocolate has melted, stirring occasionally. Remove from the heat and let cool for 30 minutes. Using an electric mixer, whip the cream until holding firm peaks. Fold in the chocolate. Cover and chill in the refrigerator for 30–45 minutes until firm enough to spread.

To assemble, spread the white chocolate filling on the flat side of half the cakes. Top with the rest of the cakes. Sprinkle the chocolate sprinkles over the cream edges of each whoopie pie.

caramel fudge whoopie pies

makes 10

generous 1¾ cups all-purpose flour

2 tsp baking powder

large pinch of salt

½ cup butter, softened

scant ½ cup dark brown sugar

2 tbsp dark corn syrup

1 large egg, beaten

1 tsp vanilla extract

½ cup milk

1 oz/25 g fudge, finely chopped

caramel frosting

generous ½ cup unsalted butter, softened

1 cup confectioners' sugar

5 tbsp dulce du leche (caramel)

Preheat the oven to 350°F/180°C. Line 2–3 large cookie sheets with parchment paper. Sift together the all-purpose flour, baking powder, and salt.

Place the butter and sugar in a large bowl and beat with an electric mixer until pale and fluffy. Beat in the dark corn syrup, egg, and vanilla extract followed by half of the flour mixture and then the milk. Stir in the rest of the flour mixture and mix until thoroughly incorporated.

Pipe or spoon 20 mounds of the batter onto the prepared cookie sheets, spaced well apart to allow for spreading. Bake, one sheet at a time, in the preheated oven for 10–12 minutes until risen and just firm to the touch. Cool for 5 minutes, then using a palette knife transfer to a cooling rack and let cool completely.

For the frosting, place the butter in a bowl and beat with an electric mixer for 2–3 minutes until pale and creamy. Gradually beat in the confectioners' sugar and continue beating for 2–3 minutes until the buttercream is very light and fluffy. Stir in the dulce du leche.

To assemble, spread two-thirds of the frosting on the flat side of half of the cakes. Thinly spread the rest of the frosting on the tops of the remaining cakes. Sandwich the cakes together and decorate with the chopped fudge.

chocolate & lime whoopie pies

makes 10

generous 1¾ cups all-purpose flour

1 tsp baking soda

¼ cup unsweetened cocoa

large pinch of salt

½ cup butter, softened

¾ cup superfine sugar

1 large egg, beaten

1 tsp vanilla extract

4 tbsp sour cream

3 tbsp milk

chocolate icing

3 oz/85 g semisweet chocolate, broken into pieces

4 tbsp unsalted butter

lime cream cheese filling

¾ cup cream cheese

5 tbsp unsalted butter, softened

juice and finely grated rind of 1 lime

1 cup confectioners' sugar, sifted

Preheat the oven to 350°F/180°C. Line 2–3 large cookie sheets with parchment paper. Sift together the all-purpose flour, baking soda, unsweetened cocoa, and salt.

Place the butter and sugar in a large bowl and beat with an electric mixer until pale and fluffy. Beat in the egg and vanilla extract followed by half of the flour mixture and then the sour cream and milk. Stir in the rest of the flour mixture and mix until thoroughly incorporated.

Pipe or spoon 20 mounds of the batter onto the prepared cookie sheets, spaced well apart to allow for spreading. Bake in the preheated oven, one sheet at a time, for 10–12 minutes until risen and just firm to the touch. Cool for 5 minutes, then using a palette knife transfer to a cooling rack and let cool completely.

For the icing, place the chocolate and butter in a heatproof bowl set over a pan of simmering water and heat until melted, stirring occasionally. Remove from the heat and let cool for 20 minutes, stirring occasionally.

For the filling, place the cream cheese, butter, and lime juice and rind in a bowl and beat with an electric mixer until smooth. Gradually beat in the confectioners' sugar.

To assemble, spread the lime filling on the flat side of half the cakes. Top with the rest of the cakes. Gently dip one half of each whoopie pie in the chocolate icing and place on a cooling rack set over a baking sheet. Place in the refrigerator for 20 minutes until the icing has just set.

malted milk whoopie pies

makes 25

1²/₃ cup all-purpose flour

1 tsp baking soda

large pinch of salt

4 tbsp malted milk powder

½ cup butter, softened

scant ½ cup superfine sugar

scant ¼ cup light brown sugar

1 large egg, beaten

1 tsp vanilla extract

4 tbsp sour cream

3 tbsp milk

3 tbsp mini candy-coated chocolates, to decorate

vanilla buttercream filling

6 tbsp unsalted butter, softened

1 tsp vanilla extract

5 tbsp heavy cream

2½ cups confectioners' sugar, sifted

icing

1½ cups confectioners' sugar

2–3 tbsp warm water

red, green, and yellow liquid food coloring

Preheat the oven to 350°F/180°C. Line 2–3 large cookie sheets with parchment paper. Sift together the all-purpose flour, baking soda, and salt. Stir in the malted milk powder.

Place the butter and sugars in a large bowl and beat with an electric mixer until pale and fluffy. Beat in the egg and vanilla extract followed by half of the flour mixture and then the sour cream and milk. Stir in the rest of the flour mixture and beat until thoroughly incorporated.

Pipe or spoon 50 small mounds of the batter onto the prepared cookie sheets, spaced well apart to allow for spreading. Bake in the preheated oven, one sheet at a time, for 8–10 minutes until risen and just firm to the touch. Cool for 5 minutes, then using a palette knife transfer to a cooling rack and let cool completely.

For the filling, place the butter and vanilla extract in a bowl and beat with an electric mixer for 2–3 minutes until pale and creamy. Beat in the cream, then gradually beat in the confectioners' sugar and continue beating for 2–3 minutes until the buttercream is very light and fluffy.

For the icing, sift the confectioners' sugar into a bowl and stir in enough water to make a smooth icing that is thick enough to coat the back of a wooden spoon. Divide the icing between three small bowls and beat in a few drops of red, green, or yellow coloring to each bowl.

To assemble, spread or pipe the buttercream on the flat side of half of the cakes. Top with the rest of the cakes. Spoon the icing over the whoopie pies and decorate with the candy-coated chocolates. Let set.

Gourmet Whoopie

marbled mocha whoopie pies

makes 10

generous 1¾ cups all-purpose flour

1 tsp baking soda

large pinch of salt

½ cup butter, softened

¾ cup superfine sugar

1 large egg, beaten

⅔ cup buttermilk

1 tsp vanilla extract

1 tsp cold strong black coffee or coffee extract

1 tbsp unsweetened cocoa

chocolate & cream filling

5 oz/140 g semisweet chocolate, finely chopped

generous 1¾ cups heavy cream

1 tbsp cold strong black coffee

Preheat the oven to 350°F/180°C. Line 2–3 large cookie sheets with parchment paper. Sift together the all-purpose flour, baking soda, and salt.

Place the butter and sugar in a large bowl and beat with an electric mixer until pale and fluffy. Beat in the egg followed by half of the flour mixture and then the buttermilk. Reserving 1 tablespoon, stir in the rest of the flour mixture and mix until thoroughly incorporated.

Transfer half the batter to a second bowl. Stir the vanilla extract and remaining tablespoon of flour batter into one bowl. Stir the coffee or coffee extract and unsweetened cocoa into the second bowl. Gently swirl the two batter together to create a marbled effect.

Pipe or spoon 20 mounds of the batter onto the prepared cookie sheets, spaced well apart to allow for spreading. Bake in the preheated oven, one sheet at a time, for 10–12 minutes until risen and just firm to the touch. Cool for 5 minutes, then using a palette knife transfer to a cooling rack and let cool completely.

For the filling, place the chocolate in a heatproof bowl. Heat a scant 1 cup of the cream and the coffee in a small heavy-bottom saucepan until boiling, then pour over the chocolate and stir until the chocolate has melted. Let cool for 20–30 minutes, stirring occasionally, until thickened. Beat the rest of the cream until it holds firm peaks.

To assemble, spread the chocolate mixture on the flat side of half of the cakes and top with the whipped cream. Top with the rest of the cakes.

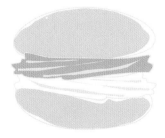

black forest whoopie pies

makes 10

generous 1¾ cups all-purpose flour

1 tsp baking soda

¼ cup unsweetened cocoa

large pinch of salt

½ cup butter, softened

¾ cup light brown sugar

1 large egg, beaten

1 tsp vanilla extract

4 tbsp sour cream

3 tbsp milk

⅓ cup chopped, dried cherries

unsweetened cocoa, to dust

filling

1¼ cups heavy cream

2 tbsp cherry liqueur (optional)

6 tbsp cherry conserve

2 oz/55 g semisweet chocolate, grated

Preheat the oven to 350°F/180°C. Line 2–3 large cookie sheets with parchment paper. Sift together the all-purpose flour, baking soda, unsweetened cocoa, and salt.

Place the butter and sugar in a large bowl and beat with an electric mixer until pale and fluffy. Beat in the egg and vanilla extract followed by half of the flour mixture and then the sour cream and milk. Stir in the rest of the flour mixture and mix until thoroughly incorporated. Stir in the chopped dried cherries.

Pipe or spoon 20 mounds of the batter onto the prepared cookie sheets, spaced well apart to allow for spreading. Bake in the preheated oven, one sheet at a time, for 10–12 minutes until risen and just firm to the touch. Cool for 5 minutes, then using a palette knife transfer to a cooling rack and let cool completely.

For the filling, place the cream and cherry liqueur (if using) in a bowl and beat until it holds firm peaks.

To assemble, spread the cherry conserve on the flat side of half the cakes. Top with the whipped cream and the grated chocolate. Top with the rest of the cakes. Dust lightly with unsweetened cocoa.

pistachio & honey whoopie pies

makes 12

generous 1¾ cups all-purpose flour

1 tsp baking soda

large pinch of salt

¾ cup pistachios, finely ground plus 1 tbsp chopped

½ cup butter, softened

¾ cup superfine sugar

finely grated rind of ½ lemon

1 large egg, beaten

⅔ cup buttermilk

honey mascarpone filling

1 cup mascarpone cheese

½ cup heavy cream

4 tbsp dark honey

Preheat the oven to 350°F/180°C. Line 2–3 large cookie sheets with parchment paper. Sift together the all-purpose flour, baking soda, and salt. Stir in the ground pistachios.

Place the butter, sugar and lemon rind in a large bowl and beat with an electric mixer until pale and fluffy. Beat in the egg, followed by half of the flour mixture and then the buttermilk. Stir in the rest of the flour mixture and mix until thoroughly incorporated.

Pipe or spoon 24 mounds of the batter onto the prepared cookie sheets, spaced well apart to allow for spreading. Sprinkle with the chopped pistachios. Bake, one sheet at a time, in the preheated oven for 10–12 minutes until risen and just firm to the touch. Cool for 5 minutes, then using a palette knife transfer to a cooling rack and let cool completely.

For the filling, place the mascarpone and cream in a bowl and beat until smooth. Stir in the honey. Chill for 30 minutes.

To assemble, spread the mascarpone cream on the flat side of half of the cakes. Top with the rest of the cakes.

strawberry & cream whoopie pies

makes 12

generous 1¾ cups all-purpose
flour

1 tsp baking soda

large pinch of salt

½ cup butter, softened

¾ cup superfine sugar

1 large egg, beaten

2 tsp rose flower water

⅔ cup buttermilk

confectioners' sugar, to dust

filling

1¼ cups heavy cream

4 tbsp confectioners' sugar, sifted

3 tbsp strawberry jelly

1⅓ cups sliced strawberries

Preheat the oven to 350°F/180°C. Line 2–3 large cookie sheets with parchment paper. Sift together the all-purpose flour, baking soda, and salt.

Place the butter and sugar in a large bowl and beat with an electric mixer until pale and fluffy. Beat in the egg and rose flower water, followed by half of the flour mixture and then the buttermilk. Stir in the rest of the flour mixture and mix until thoroughly incorporated.

Pipe or spoon 24 mounds of the batter onto the prepared cookie sheets, spaced well apart to allow for spreading. Bake in the preheated oven, one sheet at a time, for 10–12 minutes until risen and just firm to the touch. Cool for 5 minutes, then using a palette knife transfer to a cooling rack and let cool completely.

For the filling, place the cream in a bowl and beat until it holds firm peaks. Fold in the sifted confectioners' sugar.

To assemble, spread the strawberry jelly on the flat side of half of the cakes. Top with the cream and strawberries. Top with the rest of the cakes. Dust with confectioners' sugar.

spiced carrot & orange whoopie pies

makes 10

generous 1¾ cups whole wheat flour

2 tsp baking powder

large pinch of salt

1½ tsp allspice

4 tbsp butter, softened

¼ cup vegetable shortening

¾ cup light brown sugar

1 large egg, beaten

generous ⅓ cup milk

1¼ cups finely grated carrots

¼ cup walnuts, chopped

4 oz/115 g ready-to-roll fondant

orange and green food coloring paste

orange filling

1 cup cream cheese

½ cup unsalted butter, softened

finely grated rind and 2 tbsp juice from 1 orange

1¾ cups confectioners' sugar

1 tsp allspice

Preheat the oven to 350°F/180°C. Line 2–3 large cookie sheets with parchment paper. Sift together the whole wheat flour, baking powder, salt, and allspice, tipping any bran left in the sifter into the bowl.

Place the butter, vegetable shortening and sugar in a large bowl and beat with an electric mixer until pale and fluffy. Beat in the egg followed by half of the flour mixture and then the milk. Stir in the rest of the flour mixture and mix until thoroughly incorporated. Stir in the carrots and walnuts.

Pipe or spoon 20 mounds of the batter onto the prepared cookie sheets, spaced well apart to allow for spreading. Bake, one sheet at a time, in the preheated oven for 10–12 minutes until risen and just firm to the touch. Cool for 5 minutes, then using a palette knife transfer to a cooling rack and let cool completely.

For the filling, place the cream cheese, butter and orange rind and juice in a bowl and beat with an electric mixer for 2–3 minutes until pale and creamy. Gradually beat in the confectioners' sugar and allspice until smooth.

To assemble, spread or pipe the orange filling on the flat side of half of the cakes. Top with the rest of the cakes. Color three-quarters of the fondant orange and the rest green and shape into 10 mini carrots with leaves. Place one on top of each whoopie pie.

hazelnut praline whoopie pies

makes 10

generous 1¾ cups all-purpose flour

1 tsp baking soda

large pinch of salt

½ cup butter, softened

¾ cup dark brown sugar

1 large egg, beaten

⅔ cup buttermilk

½ cup chopped hazelnuts, lightly toasted

praline buttercream filling

⅔ cup superfine sugar

⅓ cup chopped hazelnuts

¾ cup unsalted butter, softened

1½ cups confectioners' sugar, sifted

Preheat the oven to 350°F/180°C. Line 2–3 large cookie sheets with parchment paper. Sift together the all-purpose flour, baking soda, and salt.

Place the butter and sugar in a large bowl and beat with an electric mixer until pale and fluffy. Beat in the egg, followed by half of the flour mixture and then the buttermilk. Stir in the rest of the flour mixture and mix until thoroughly incorporated. Fold in the chopped hazelnuts.

Pipe or spoon 20 mounds of the batter onto the prepared cookie sheets, spaced well apart to allow for spreading. Bake, one sheet at a time, in the preheated oven for 10–12 minutes until risen and just firm to the touch. Cool for 5 minutes, then using a palette knife transfer to a cooling rack and let cool completely.

For the filling, place the sugar in a heavy-bottom saucepan and heat gently until dissolved. Continue cooking, without stirring and occasionally swirling the pan, until the liquid has turned to a deep golden caramel. Spread the chopped hazelnuts on a nonstick baking sheet and quickly pour the hot caramel over the nuts. Let stand until cold and set. Break the praline into smaller pieces and crush with a toffee hammer or in a food processor.

Place the butter in a bowl and beat with an electric mixer for 2–3 minutes until pale and creamy. Gradually beat in the confectioners' sugar and beat for 2–3 minutes. Stir in two-thirds of the crushed praline.

To assemble, spread the buttercream on the flat side of half of the cakes. Top with the rest of the cakes. Spread the remaining praline on a plate and roll the edges of each whoopie pie in the praline to coat.

after dinner mint whoopie pies

makes 30

1¼ cups all-purpose flour

1½ tsp baking soda

scant ½ cup unsweetened cocoa

large pinch of salt

6 tbsp butter, softened

generous ⅓ cup vegetable shortening

¾ cup light brown sugar

1 large egg, beaten

⅔ cup milk

mint filling

1¼ cups cream cheese

¾ cup unsalted butter, softened

2½ tsp of peppermint extract

1½ cups confectioners' sugar, sifted, plus extra for dusting

few drops green food coloring

Preheat the oven to 350°F/180°C. Line 2–3 large cookie sheets with parchment paper. Sift together the all-purpose flour, baking soda, unsweetened cocoa, and salt.

Place the butter, vegetable shortening, and sugar in a large bowl and beat with an electric mixer until pale and fluffy. Beat in the egg followed by half of the flour mixture and then the milk. Stir in the rest of the flour mixture and mix until thoroughly incorporated.

Pipe or spoon 60 small mounds of the batter onto the prepared cookie sheets, spaced well apart to allow for spreading. Bake in the preheated oven, one sheet at a time, for 8–10 minutes until risen and just firm to the touch. Cool for 5 minutes, then using a palette knife transfer to a cooling rack and let cool completely.

For the filling, place the cream cheese and butter in a bowl and beat together until well blended. Beat in the peppermint extract and confectioners' sugar until smooth. Transfer half the mixture to a second bowl and stir in a few drops of food coloring to create a pale green color. Chill both fillings in the refrigerator for 30 minutes.

To assemble, carefully spoon the two fillings alternately into a piping bag fitted with a star-shaped nozzle. Pipe swirls of the filling onto the flat side of half the cakes. Top with the rest of the cakes and dust with confectioners' sugar.

snickerdoodle whoopie pies

makes 15

generous 1¾ cups all-purpose flour

1 tsp baking soda

large pinch of salt

2 tsp ground cinnamon

½ cup butter, softened

¾ cup plus 2 tbsp superfine sugar

1 large egg, beaten

1 tsp vanilla extract

⅔ cup buttermilk

coffee filling

½ cup unsalted butter, softened

scant ½ cup cream cheese

1 tbsp strong cold black coffee

2½ cups confectioners' sugar, sifted

Preheat the oven to 350°F/180°C. Line 2–3 large cookie sheets with parchment paper. Sift together the all-purpose flour, baking soda, salt, and 1 teaspoon of cinnamon.

Place the butter and the ¾ cup superfine sugar in a large bowl and beat with an electric mixer until pale and fluffy. Beat in the egg and vanilla extract followed by half of the flour mixture and then the buttermilk. Stir in the rest of the flour mixture and mix until thoroughly incorporated.

Pipe or spoon 30 mounds of the batter onto the prepared cookie sheets, spaced well apart to allow for spreading. Mix together the rest of the cinnamon with the 2 tablespoons of superfine sugar and sprinkle liberally over the mounds. Bake in the preheated oven, one sheet at a time, for 10–12 minutes until risen and just firm to the touch. Cool for 5 minutes, then using a palette knife transfer to a cooling rack and let cool completely.

For the filling, place the butter, cream cheese, and coffee in a bowl and beat together until well blended. Gradually beat in the confectioners' sugar until smooth.

To assemble, spread or pipe the coffee filling on the flat side of half of the cakes. Top with the rest of the cakes.

Party Whoopie

tutti frutti whoopie pies

makes 25

generous 1¾ cups all-purpose flour

1 tsp baking soda

large pinch of salt

½ cup butter, softened

¾ cup superfine sugar

1 large egg, beaten

½ tsp vanilla extract

⅔ cup buttermilk

½ cup finely chopped mixed colored candied cherries

4 tbsp multicolored sugar sprinkles

marshmallow filling

8oz/225 g white marshmallows

4 tbsp milk

few drops red food coloring

½ cup vegetable shortening

½ cup confectioners' sugar, sifted

Preheat the oven to 350°F/180°C. Line 2–3 large cookie sheets with parchment paper. Sift together the all-purpose flour, baking soda, and salt.

Place the butter and sugar in a large bowl and beat with an electric mixer until pale and fluffy. Beat in the egg and vanilla extract followed by half of the flour mixture and then the buttermilk. Stir in the rest of the flour mixture and mix until thoroughly incorporated. Stir in the chopped cherries.

Pipe or spoon 50 small mounds of the batter onto the prepared cookie sheets, spaced well apart to allow for spreading. Bake in the preheated oven, one sheet at a time, for 9–11 minutes until risen and just firm to the touch. Cool for 5 minutes, then using a palette knife transfer to a cooling rack and let cool completely.

For the filling, place the marshmallows, milk, and food coloring in a heatproof bowl set over a pan of simmering water. Heat until the marshmallows have melted, stirring occasionally. Remove from the heat and let cool.

Place the vegetable shortening and confectioners' sugar in a bowl and beat together until smooth and creamy. Add the creamed mixture to the marshmallow and beat for 1–2 minutes until fluffy.

To assemble, spread the filling over the flat side of half the cakes. Top with the remaining cakes. Roll the edges of the pies in the sugar sprinkles.

toffee nut ice cream whoopie pies

makes 12

generous 1¾ cups all-purpose flour

1 tsp baking soda

1 tsp allspice

large pinch of salt

½ cup butter, softened

¾ cup light brown sugar

1 large egg, beaten

4 tbsp sour cream

3 tbsp milk

4 tbsp chopped mixed nuts

filling

1 pint vanilla ice cream

½ cup dulce du leche (caramel)

Preheat the oven to 350°F/180°C. Line 2–3 large cookie sheets with parchment paper. Sift together the all-purpose flour, baking soda, allspice, and salt.

Place the butter and sugar in a large bowl and beat with an electric mixer until pale and fluffy. Beat in the egg followed by half of the flour mixture and then the sour cream and milk. Stir in the rest of the flour mixture and mix until thoroughly incorporated. Stir in the nuts.

Pipe or spoon 24 mounds of the batter onto the prepared cookie sheets, spaced well apart to allow for spreading. Bake in the preheated oven, one sheet at a time, for 10–12 minutes until risen and just firm to the touch. Cool for 5 minutes, then using a palette knife transfer to a cooling rack and let cool completely.

To assemble, remove the ice cream from the freezer and let soften for 15 minutes. Spread a layer of dulce du leche on half the cakes and top with a generous scoop of ice cream. Place the rest of the cakes on top, pressing down gently. Serve immediately or wrap the whoopie pies individually in plastic wrap and freeze. Remove from the freezer 30 minutes before serving.

chocolate whoopie pie birthday cake

serves 8

1¼ cups all-purpose flour

1½ tsp baking soda

scant ½ cup unsweetened cocoa

large pinch of salt

6 tbsp butter, softened

generous ⅓ cup vegetable shortening

¾ cup dark brown sugar

1 large egg, beaten

1 tsp vanilla extract

⅔ cup milk

generous ⅓ cup strawberry jelly

confectioners' sugar, to dust

birthday candles

marshmallow filling

6 oz/175 g white marshmallows

3 tbsp milk

scant 1 cup heavy cream

Preheat the oven to 350°F/180°C. Grease two 8-inch/20-cm round cake pans and line the bottoms with parchment paper. Sift together the all-purpose flour, baking soda, unsweetened cocoa, and salt.

Place the butter, vegetable shortening, and sugar in a large bowl and beat with an electric mixer until pale and fluffy. Beat in the egg and vanilla extract followed by half of the flour mixture and then the milk. Stir in the rest of the flour mixture and mix until thoroughly incorporated.

Divide the batter evenly between the prepared cake pans and gently level the surfaces. Bake in the preheated oven for 20–25 minutes until risen and just firm to the touch. Cool for 5 minutes, then using a palette knife transfer to a cooling rack and let cool completely.

For the filling, place the marshmallows and milk in a heatproof bowl set over a pan of simmering water. Heat until the marshmallows have melted, stirring occasionally. Remove from the heat and let cool.

In a separate bowl beat the cream until it holds firm peaks. Fold the cream into the marshmallow mixture. Cover and chill in the refrigerator for 30 minutes.

Sandwich the cakes together with the jelly and marshmallow cream. Dust the top of the cake with confectioners' sugar and add birthday candles to finish.

halloween whoopie pies

makes 8

generous 1¾ cups all-purpose flour

1 tsp baking soda

1½ tsp pumpkin pie spice

large pinch of salt

½ cup butter, softened

¾ light brown sugar

1 large egg, beaten

⅔ cup buttermilk

8 oz/225 g orange ready-to-use rolled fondant icing

confectioners' sugar, for dusting

4 oz/115 g black ready-to-use rolled fondant icing

tubes of yellow and black writing icing

orange buttercream filling

½ cup unsalted butter, softened

finely grated rind and juice of 1 small orange

1¾ cups confectioners' sugar, sifted

orange food coloring paste

Preheat the oven to 350°F/180°C. Line 2–3 large cookie sheets with parchment paper. Sift together the all-purpose flour, baking soda, pumpkin pie spice, and salt.

Place the butter and sugar in a large bowl and beat with an electric mixer until pale and fluffy. Beat in the egg followed by half of the flour mixture and then the buttermilk. Stir in the rest of the flour mixture and mix until thoroughly incorporated.

Pipe or spoon 16 large mounds of the batter onto the prepared cookie sheets, spaced well apart to allow for spreading. Bake in the preheated oven, one sheet at a time, for 11–13 minutes until risen and just firm to the touch. Cool for 5 minutes, then using a palette knife transfer to a cooling rack and let cool completely.

For the filling, place the butter and orange rind and juice in a bowl and beat with an electric mixer for 2–3 minutes until pale and creamy. Gradually beat in the confectioners' sugar and continue beating for 2–3 minutes until the buttercream is very light and fluffy. Beat in a little orange coloring paste to color the buttercream bright orange.

To assemble, pipe or spoon the buttercream onto the flat side of half the cakes. Top with the remaining cakes. Thinly roll the orange fondant out on a work surface dusted with confectioners' sugar and cut out eight rounds to fit the top of the cakes. Press gently onto the cakes. Roll out the black fondant and cut out four bat shapes. Place on half the cakes and use yellow writing icing to dot eyes on the bats. Use black writing icing to pipe spiderwebs on the remaining cakes.

snowflake christmas whoopie pies

makes 14

scant 1½ cups all-purpose flour

2 tsp baking powder

large pinch of salt

½ cup ground almonds

½ cup butter, softened

¾ cup superfine sugar, plus extra for sprinkling

1 large egg, beaten

1 tsp almond extract

scant ½ cup milk

1 tbsp edible silver balls

buttercream filling

6 tbsp unsalted butter, softened

½ cup heavy cream

2½ cups confectioners' sugar, sifted

icing

1 cup confectioners' sugar

1–2 tbsp warm water

Preheat the oven to 350°F/180°C. Line 2–3 large cookie sheets with parchment paper. Sift together the all-purpose flour, baking powder, and salt. Stir in the ground almonds.

Place the butter and sugar in a large bowl and beat with an electric mixer until pale and fluffy. Beat in the egg and almond extract followed by half of the flour mixture and then the milk. Stir in the rest of the flour mixture and beat until thoroughly incorporated.

Pipe or spoon 28 mounds of the batter onto the prepared cookie sheets, spaced well apart to allow for spreading. Bake in the preheated oven, one sheet at a time, for 10–12 minutes until risen and just firm to the touch. Cool for 5 minutes, then using a palette knife transfer to a cooling rack and let cool completely.

For the filling, place the butter in a bowl and beat with an electric mixer for 2–3 minutes until pale and creamy. Beat in the cream, then gradually beat in the confectioners' sugar and continue beating for 2–3 minutes until the buttercream is very light and fluffy.

For the icing, sift the confectioners' sugar into a bowl and gradually stir in enough water to make a smooth, thick icing.

To assemble, pipe or spread the buttercream on the flat side of half of the cakes. Top with the rest of the cakes. Spoon the icing into a small paper pastry bag, snip the end, and pipe snowflake patterns on the top of the whoopie pies. Decorate with silver balls and sprinkle with superfine sugar. Let set.

chocolate fudge brownie whoopie pies

makes 18

1¼ cups all-purpose flour

¾ tsp baking soda

½ cup unsweetened cocoa

pinch of salt

scant ½ cup butter, softened

generous 1 cup dark brown sugar

1 large egg, beaten

1 tsp vanilla extract

4 tbsp buttermilk

1 oz/25 g semisweet chocolate, finely chopped

¼ cup finely chopped pecans

chocolate fudge frosting

3oz/85 g semisweet chocolate, broken into pieces

4 tbsp unsalted butter

generous ½ cup light brown sugar

2 tbsp milk

1½ cups confectioners' sugar, sifted

Preheat the oven to 350°F/180°C. Line 2–3 large cookie sheets with parchment paper. Sift together the all-purpose flour, baking soda, unsweetened cocoa, and salt.

Place the butter and sugar in a large bowl and beat with an electric mixer until pale and fluffy. Beat in the egg and vanilla extract followed by half of the flour mixture and then the buttermilk. Stir in the rest of the flour mixture and mix until thoroughly incorporated. Stir in the chocolate and three-quarters of the pecans.

Using a teaspoon, place 36 small mounds of the batter onto the prepared cookie sheets, spaced well apart to allow for spreading. Bake in the preheated oven, one sheet at a time, for 8–10 minutes until risen and just firm to the touch. Cool for 5 minutes, then using a palette knife transfer to a cooling rack and let cool completely.

For the frosting, place the chocolate, butter, brown sugar, and milk in a pan and heat gently until the sugar dissolves, then bring to a boil and boil for 2–3 minutes. Remove from the heat and gradually beat in the confectioners' sugar until smooth.

To assemble, spread three-quarters of the frosting on the flat side of half the cakes. Top with the rest of the cakes. Swirl the rest of the frosting on top of the whoopie pies and decorate with the rest of the pecans.

blueberry cheesecake whoopie pies

makes 12

generous 1¾ cups all-purpose flour

1 tsp baking soda

large pinch of salt

½ cup butter, softened

¾ cup superfine sugar

1 large egg, beaten

1 tsp vanilla extract

4 tbsp sour cream

3 tbsp milk

⅓ cup sweetened dried blueberries

confectioners' sugar, to dust

lemon cheesecake filling

1 cup full fat cream cheese

2 tsp finely grated lemon rind

generous ⅓ cup sour cream

¼ cup confectioners' sugar, sifted

Preheat the oven to 350°F/180°C. Line 2–3 large cookie sheets with parchment paper. Sift together the all-purpose flour, baking soda, and salt.

Place the butter and sugar in a large bowl and beat with an electric mixer until pale and fluffy. Beat in the egg and vanilla extract followed by half of the flour mixture and then the sour cream and milk. Stir in the rest of the flour mixture and mix until thoroughly incorporated. Stir in the blueberries.

Pipe or spoon 24 mounds of the batter onto the prepared cookie sheets, spaced well apart to allow for spreading. Bake in the preheated oven, one sheet at a time, for 10–12 minutes until risen and just firm to the touch. Cool for 5 minutes, then using a palette knife transfer to a cooling rack and let cool completely.

For the filling, place the cream cheese, lemon rind, sour cream, and confectioners' sugar in a bowl and beat together until smooth.

To assemble, spread or pipe the lemon filling on the flat side of half the cakes. Top with the rest of the cakes and dust lightly with confectioners' sugar.

pina colada whoopie pies

makes 12

generous 1½ cups all-purpose flour

2 tsp baking powder

large pinch of salt

⅔ cup dry unsweetened coconut

½ cup butter, softened

¾ cup superfine sugar

1 large egg, beaten

generous ⅓ cup milk

2 tbsp finely chopped candied pineapple

toasted unsweetened coconut flakes, to decorate

rum cream filling

1¾ cups heavy cream

2 tbsp white rum

icing

1 cup confectioners' sugar

1–2 tbsp pineapple juice

Preheat the oven to 350°F/180°C. Line 2–3 large cookie sheets with parchment paper. Sift together the all-purpose flour, baking powder, and salt. Stir in the coconut.

Place the butter and sugar in a large bowl and beat with an electric mixer until pale and fluffy. Beat in the egg followed by half of the flour mixture and then the milk. Stir in the rest of the flour mixture and mix until thoroughly incorporated. Fold in the chopped pineapple.

Pipe or spoon 24 mounds of the batter onto the prepared cookie sheets, spaced well apart to allow for spreading. Bake in the preheated oven, one sheet at a time, for 10–12 minutes until risen and just firm to the touch. Cool for 5 minutes, then using a palette knife transfer to a cooling rack and let cool completely.

For the filling, place the cream and rum in a bowl and whip together until holding firm peaks.

For the icing, sift the confectioners' sugar into a bowl and gradually stir in enough pineapple juice to make a smooth icing.

To assemble, spread or pipe the rum cream on the flat side of half the cakes. Top with the rest of the cakes. Spoon the icing over the whoopie pies letting it drip down the sides. Decorate with toasted coconut. Let set.